Art

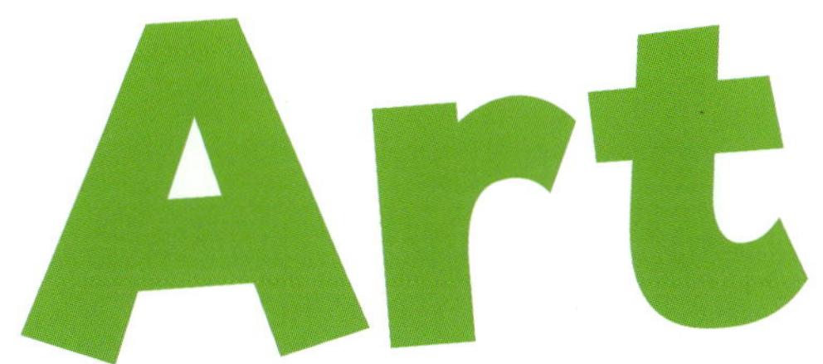

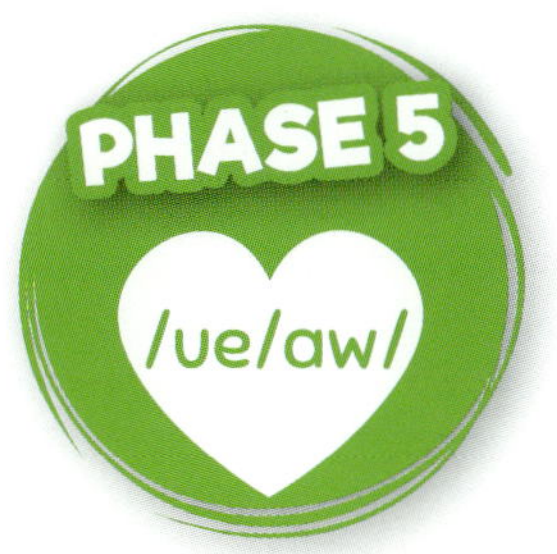

Level 5 – Green

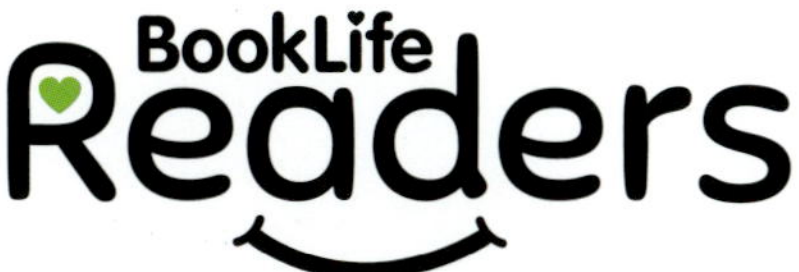

Helpful Hints for Reading at Home

The graphemes (written letters) and phonemes (units of sound) used throughout this series are aligned with Letters and Sounds. This offers a consistent approach to learning, whether reading at home or in the classroom.

HERE IS A LIST OF NEW PHONEMES FOR THIS PHASE OF LEARNING. AN EXAMPLE OF THE PRONUNCIATION CAN BE FOUND IN BRACKETS.

Phase 5			
ay (day)	ou (out)	ie (tie)	ea (eat)
oy (boy)	ir (girl)	ue (blue)	aw (saw)
wh (when)	ph (photo)	ew (new)	oe (toe)
au (Paul)	a_e (make)	e_e (these)	i_e (like)
o_e (home)	u_e (rule)		

Phase 5 Alternative Pronunciations of Graphemes			
a (hat, what)	e (bed, she)	i (fin, find)	o (hot, so, other)
u (but, unit)	c (cat, cent)	g (got, giant)	ow (cow, blow)
ie (tied, field)	ea (eat, bread)	er (farmer, herb)	ch (chin, school, chef)
y (yes, by, very)	ou (out, shoulder, could, you)		

HERE ARE SOME WORDS WHICH YOUR CHILD MAY FIND TRICKY.

Phase 5 Tricky Words			
oh	their	people	Mr
Mrs	looked	called	asked
could			

TOP TIPS FOR HELPING YOUR CHILD TO READ:

- Allow children time to break down unfamiliar words into units of sound and then encourage children to string these sounds together to create the word.

- Encourage your child to point out any focus phonics when they are used.

- Read through the book more than once to grow confidence.

- Ask simple questions about the text to assess understanding.

- Encourage children to use illustrations as prompts.

This book focuses on /ue/ and /aw/ and is a Green level 5 book band.

Can you sort all the words on this page into two groups?

Claw

Clue

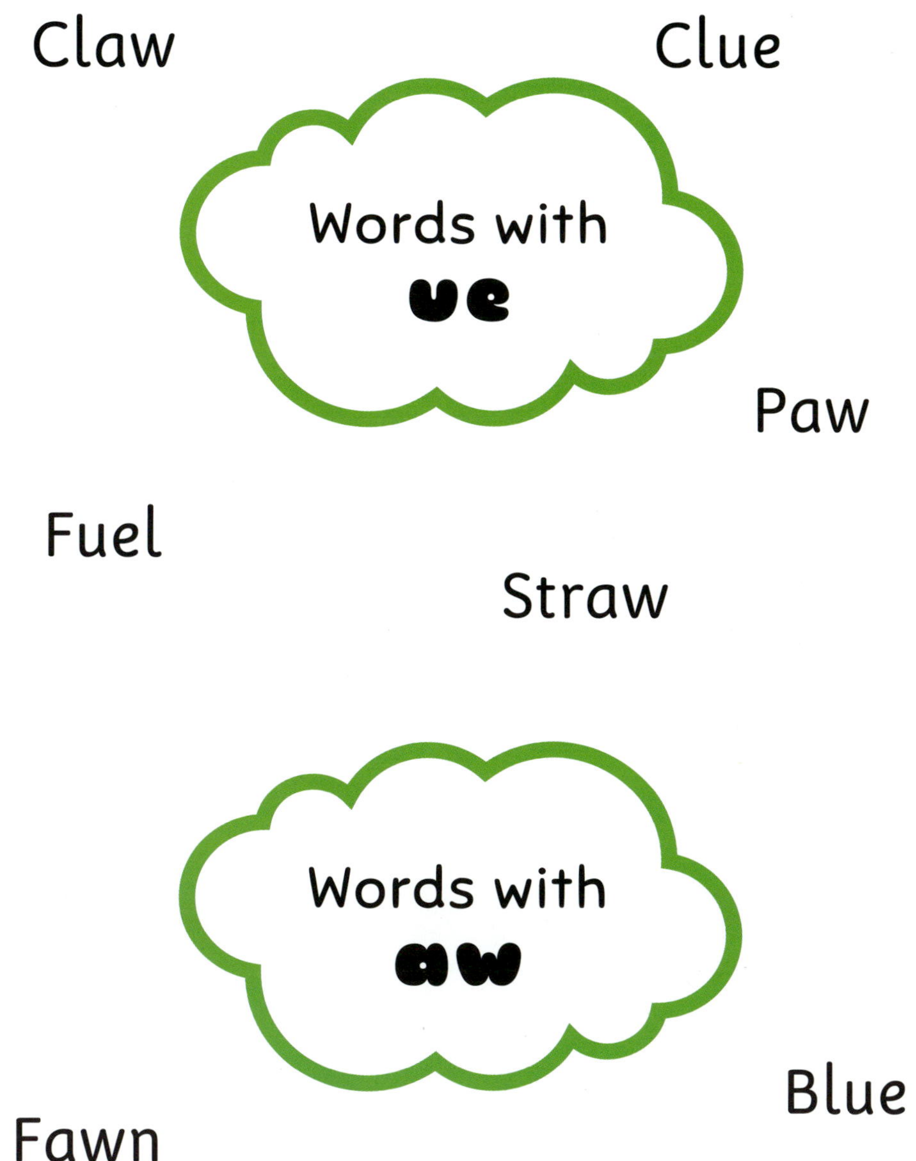

Paw

Fuel

Straw

Blue

Fawn

Do you draw, paint or enjoy art? If you do, you are an artist!

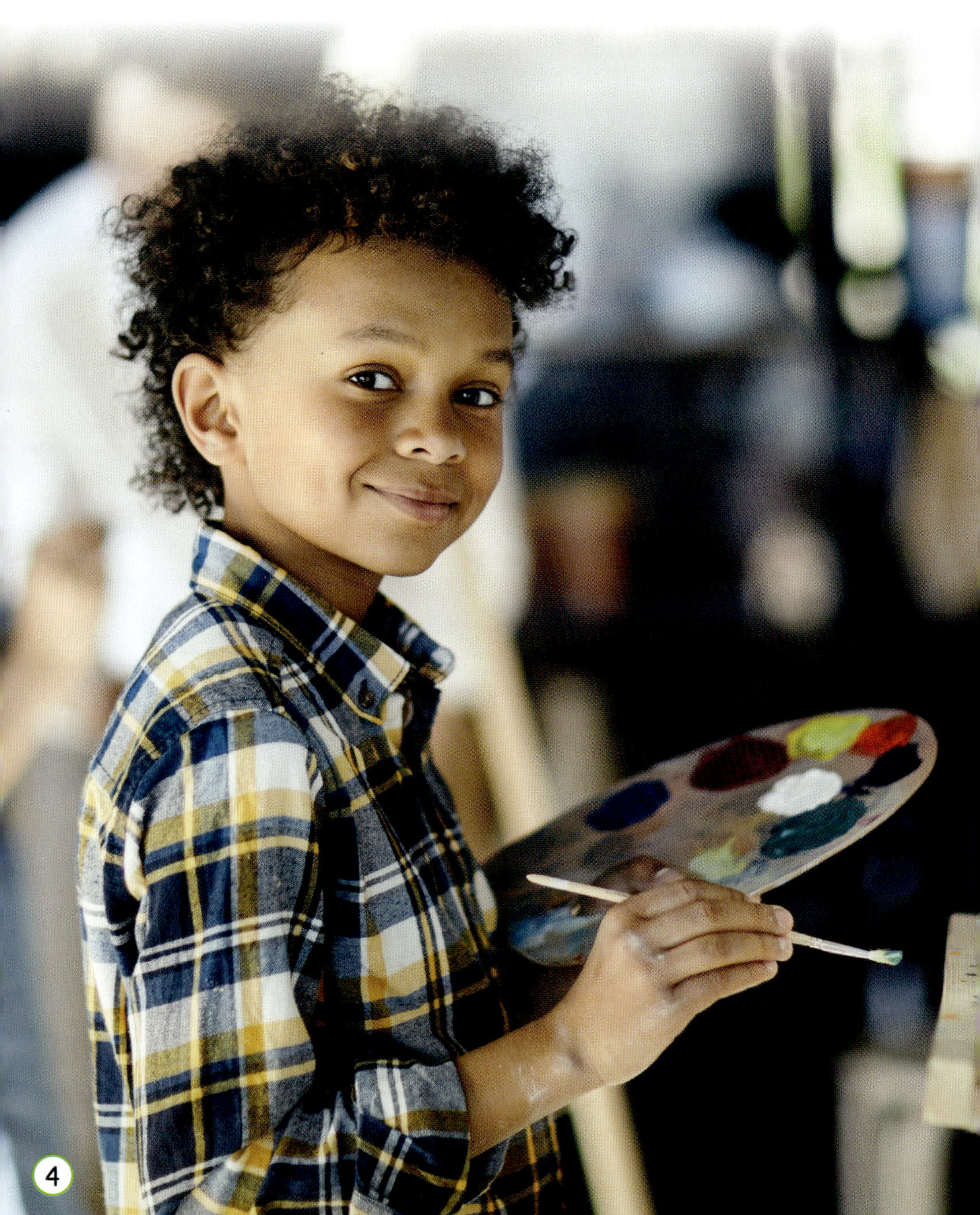

You can do art with pens, paint and glue. You can do art with lots of different things.

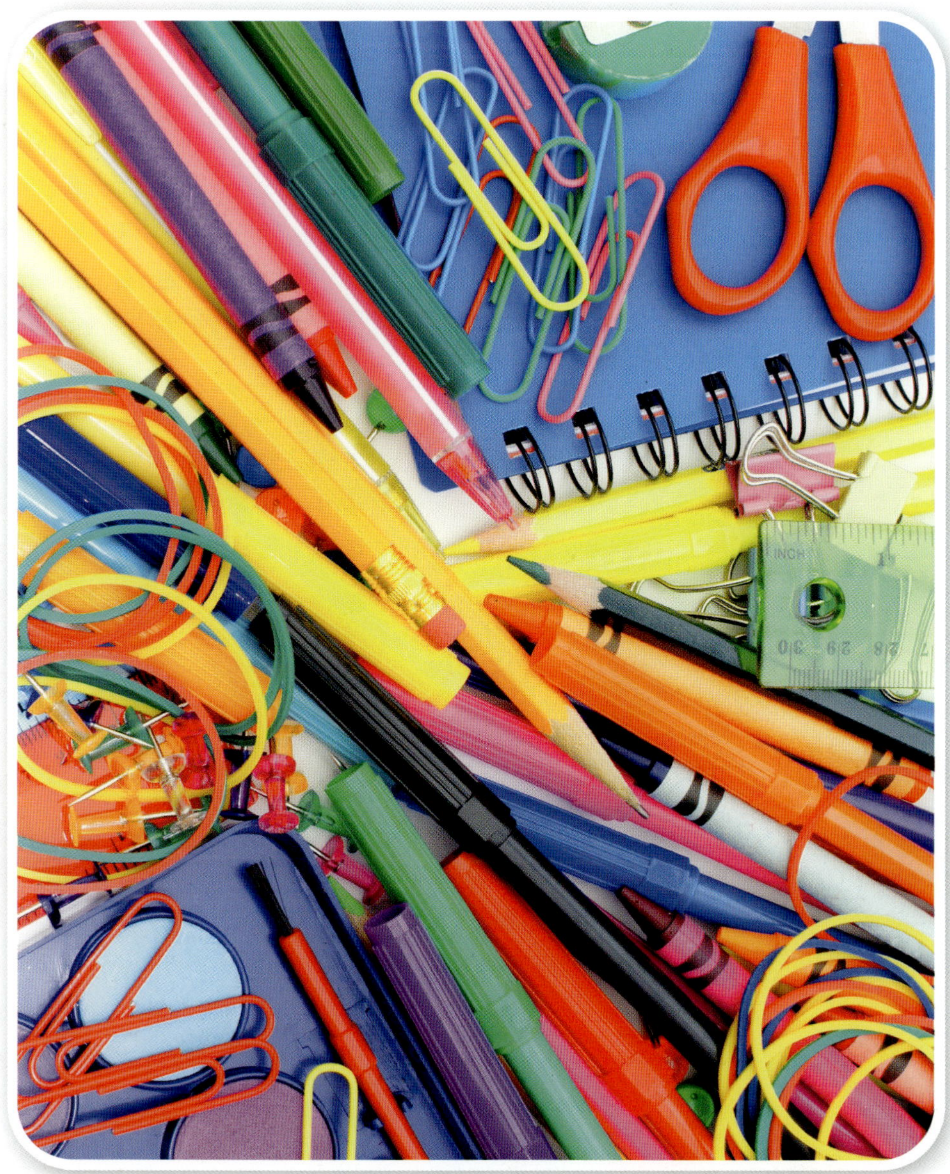

Get out all the things you need. You need a clear spot to do the art in.

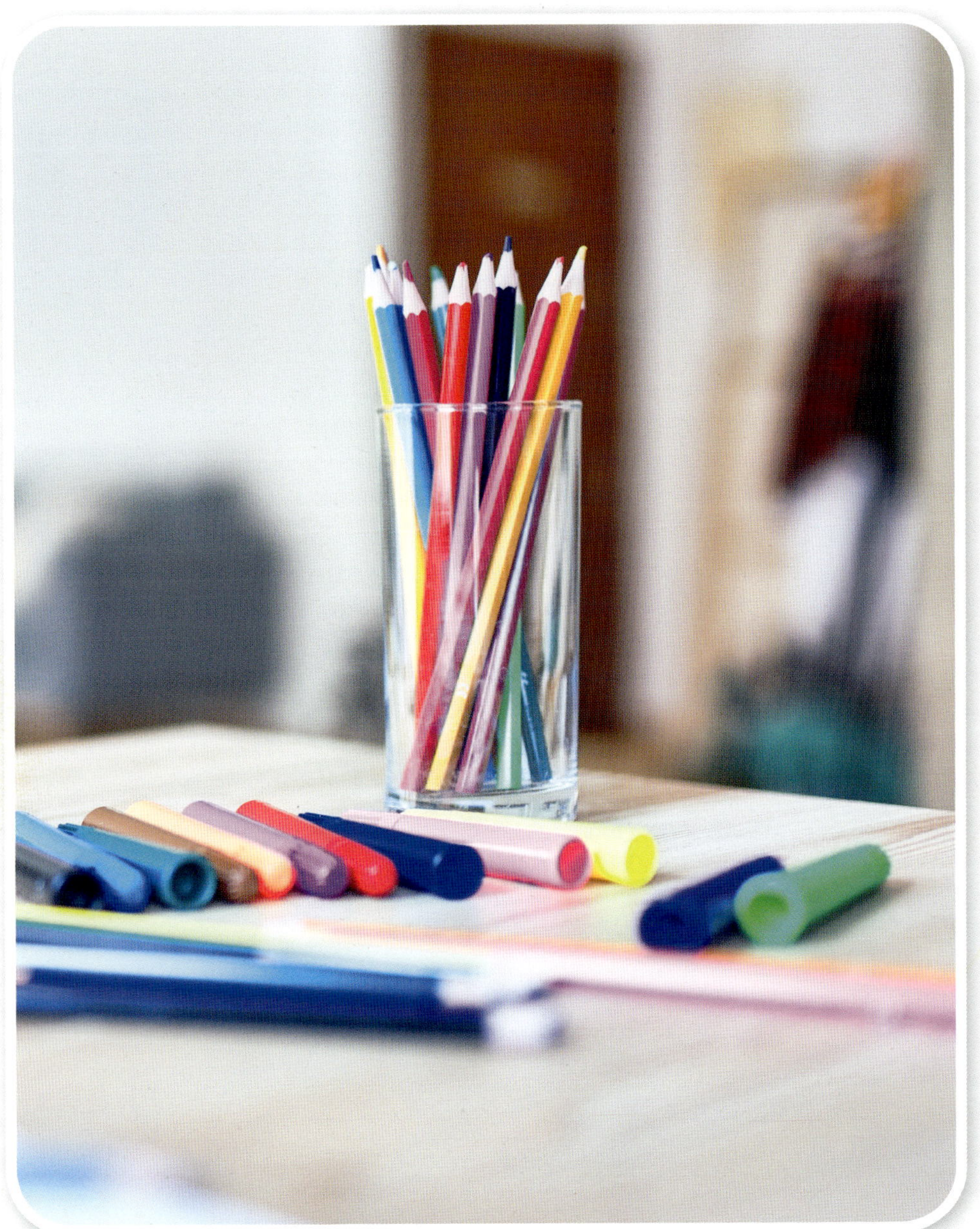

If you do not have a clue how to start, do not panic. There is no need to rush.

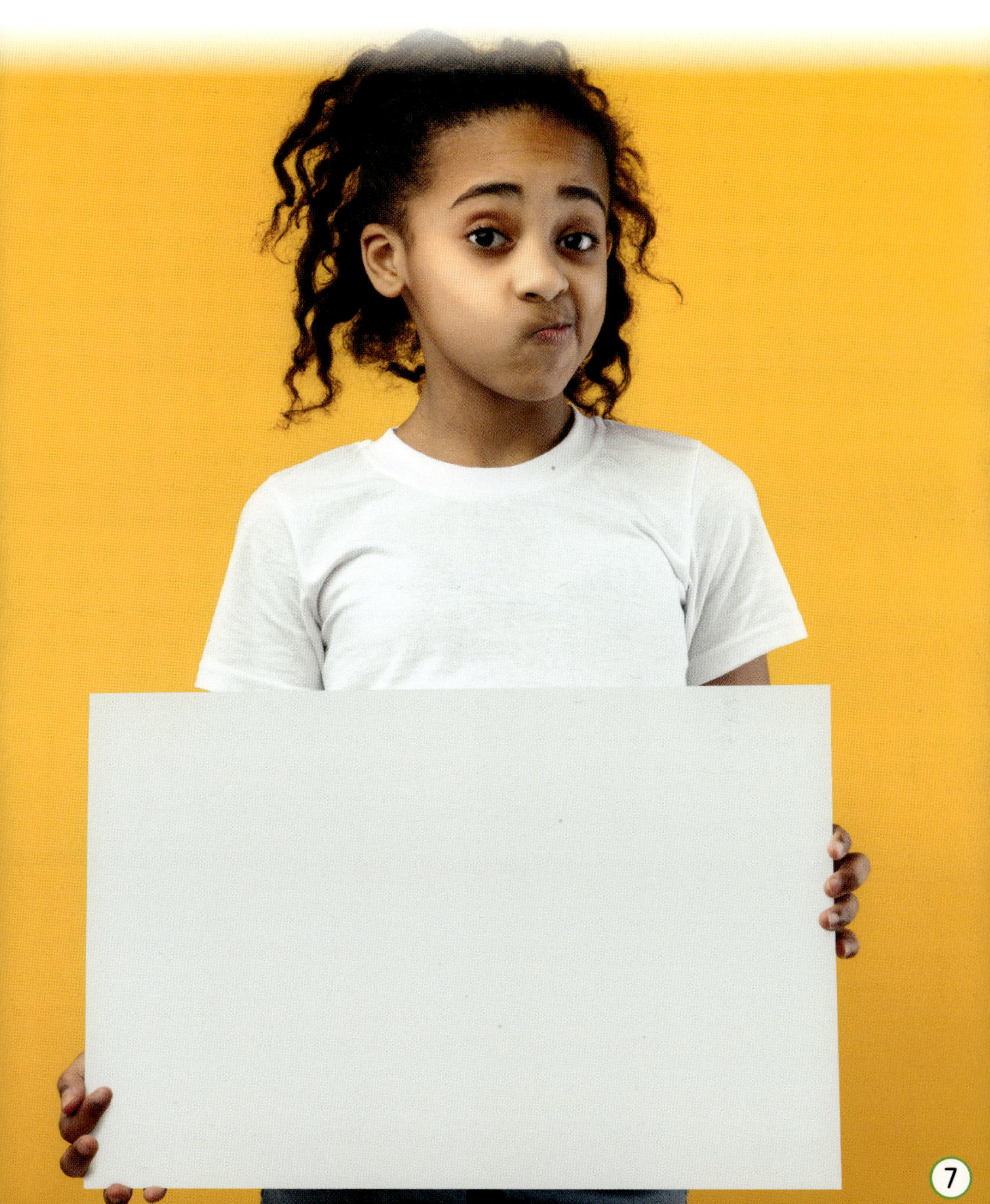

What tint could you have in the art?
Blue is a cool hue. Red is a hot hue.

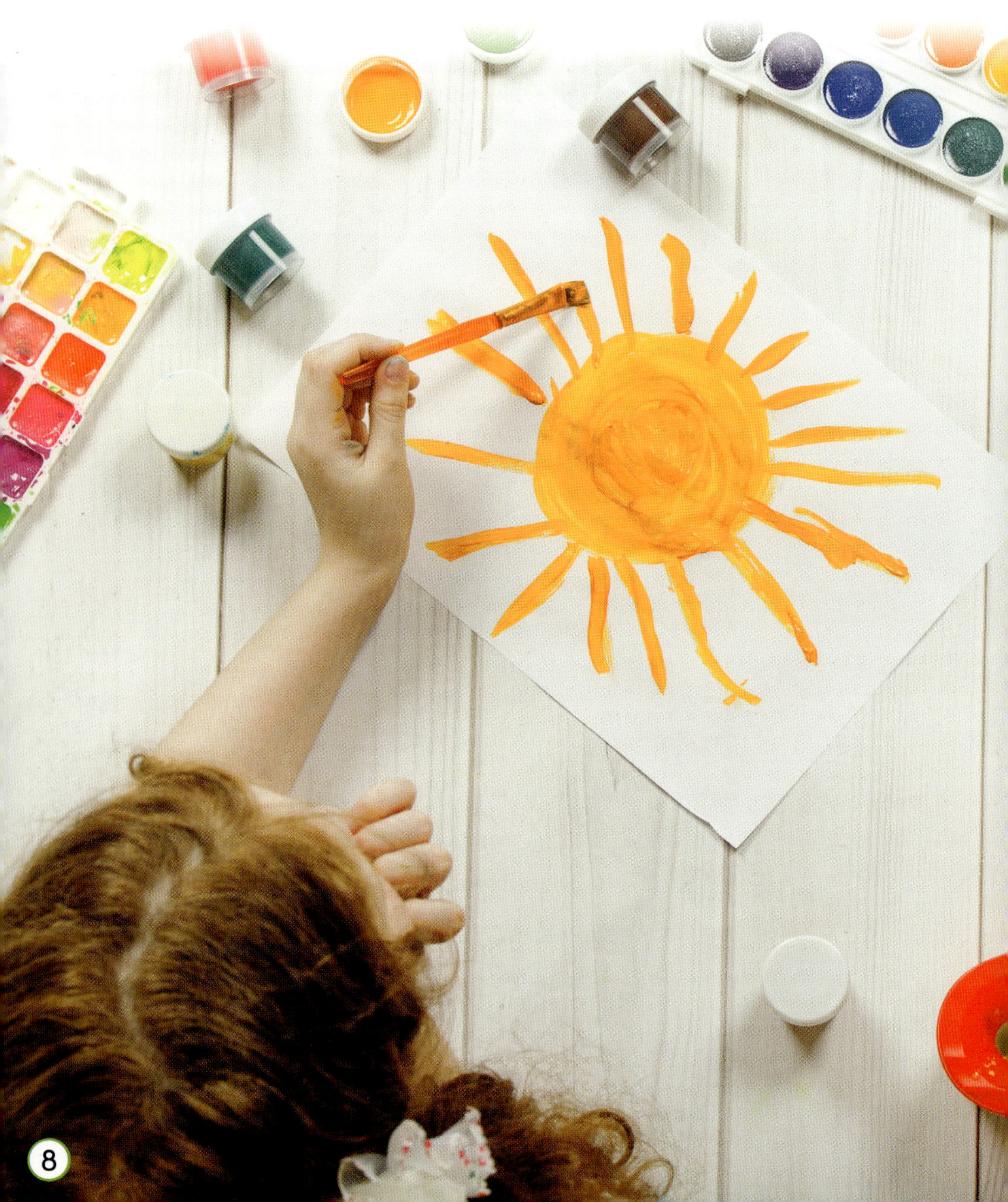

If the right hue is not there, you can mix the paint you have. You can mix a new hue.

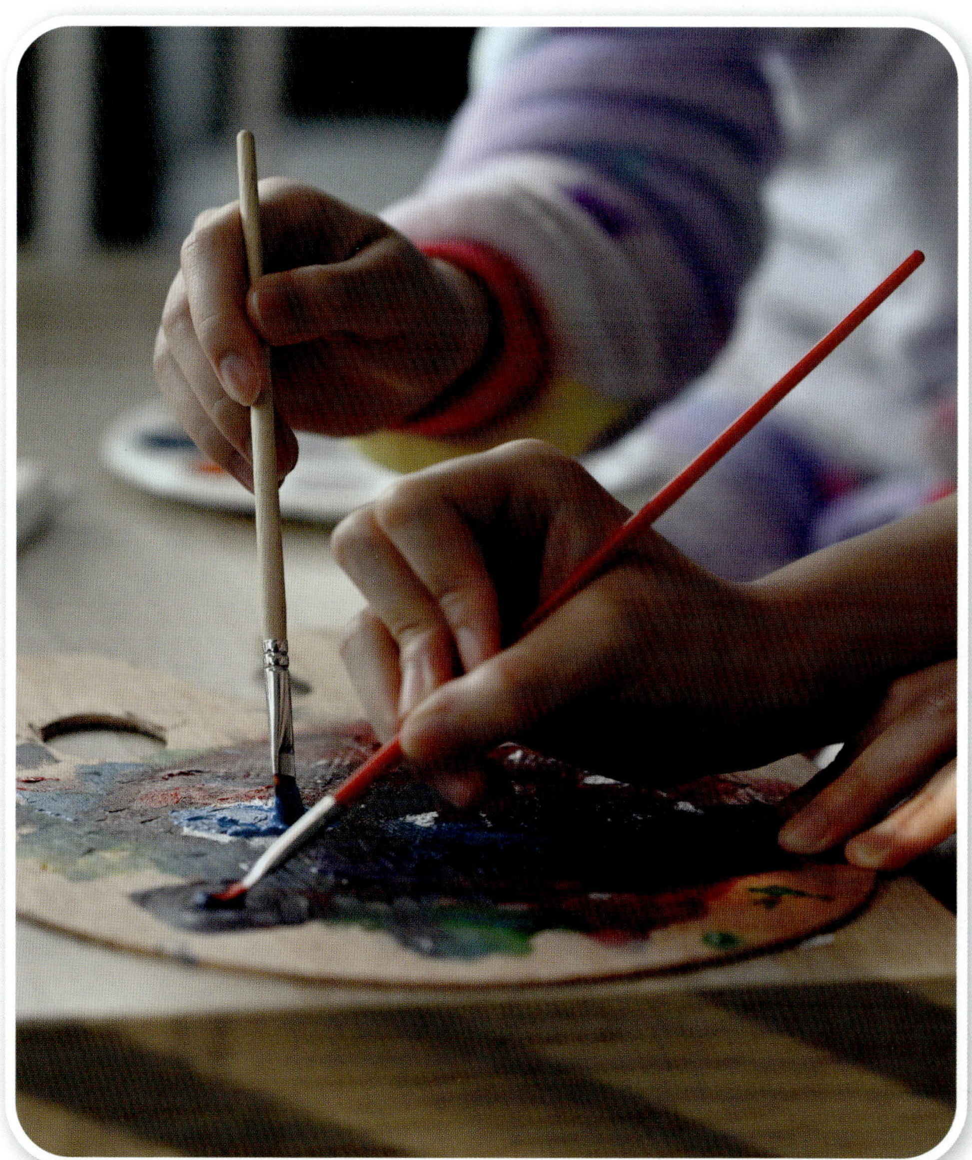

You could do a self-portrait. A self-portrait is when a person draws or paints what they look like.

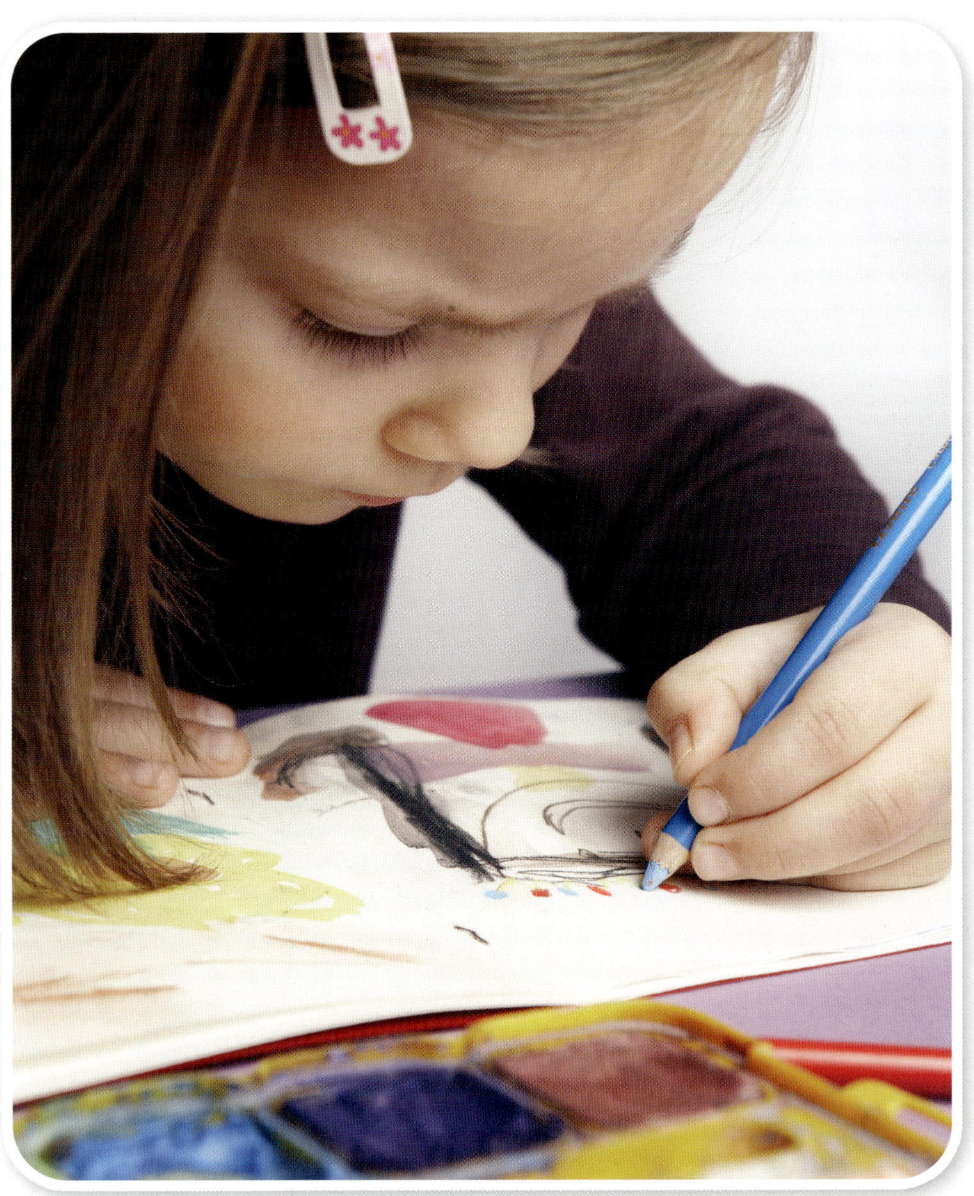

You do not have to do art of people. You could draw or paint an animal, such as a cat, dog or hawk.

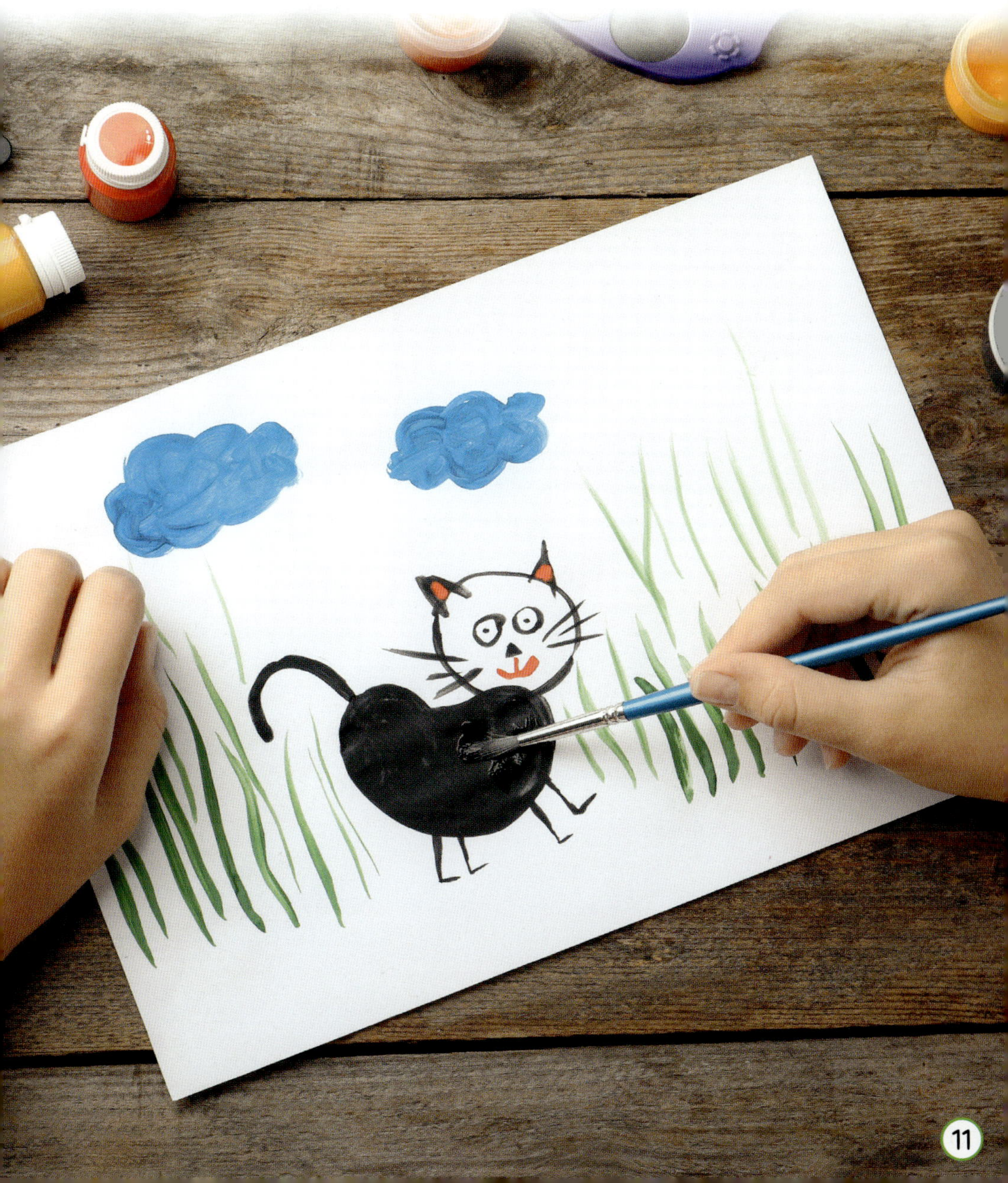

You could go out to draw or paint. Lots of people paint their town at dawn or paint a sunset.

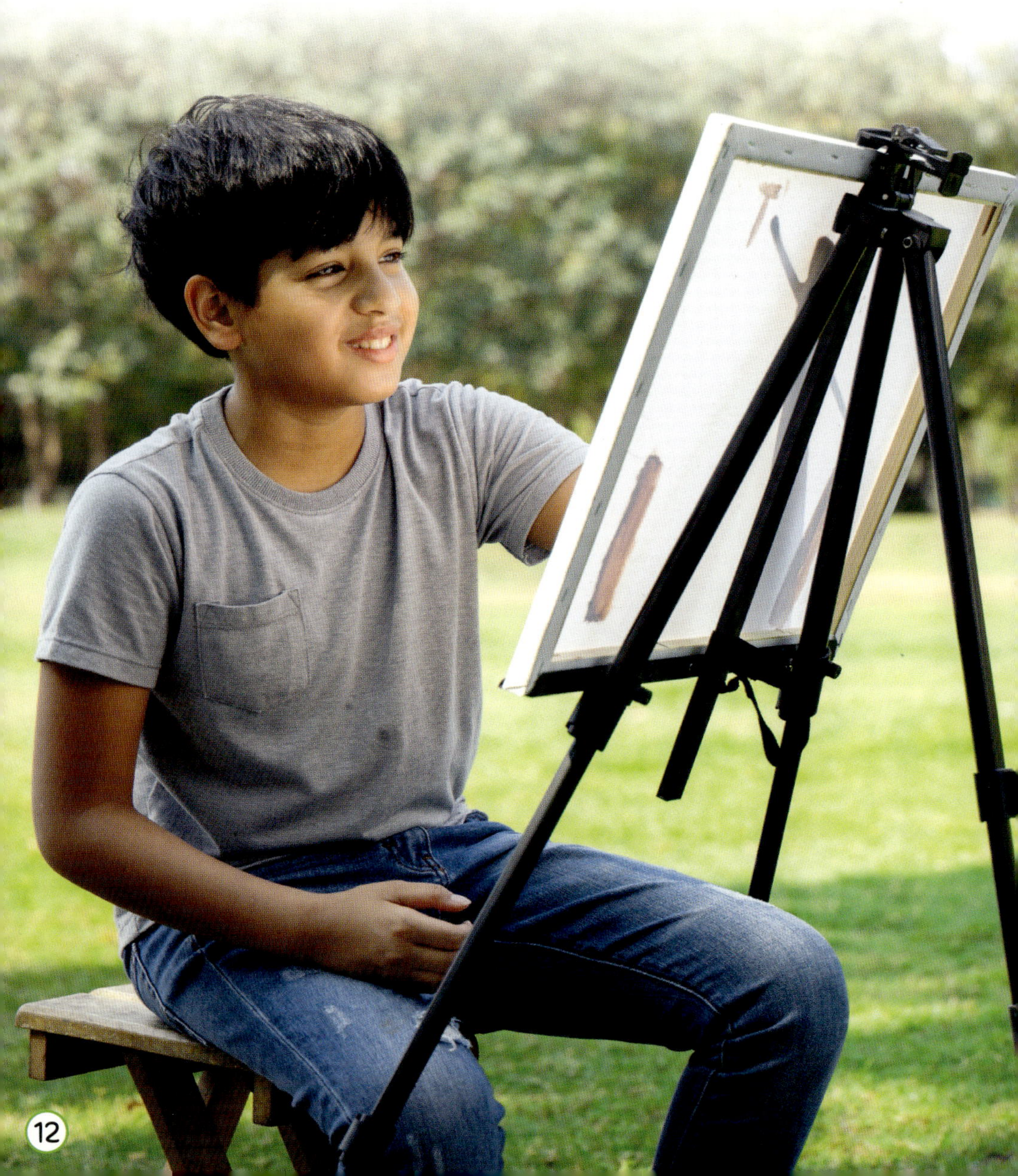

You can do art on the street. You can clean it off in a bit or wait for the rain.

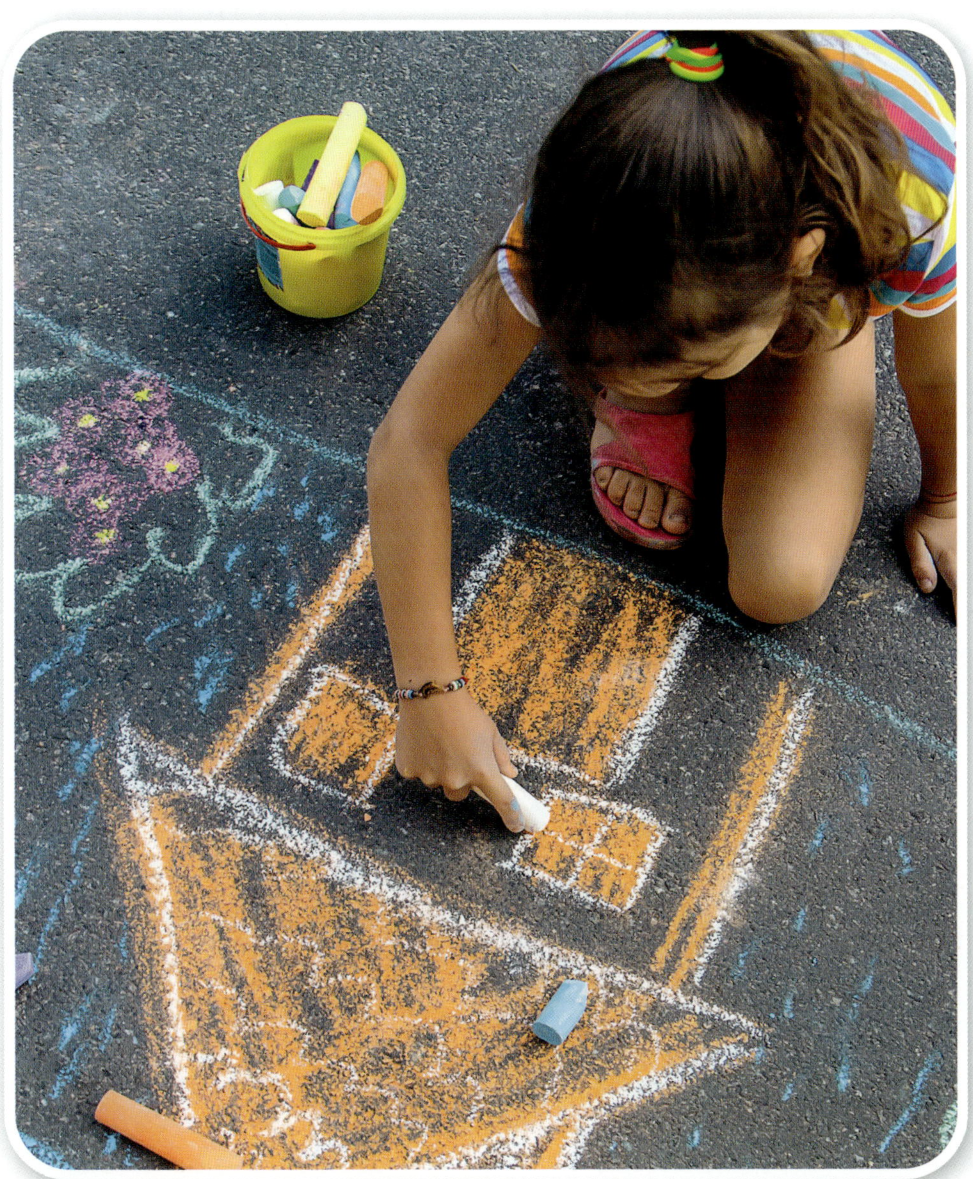

You can get junk and turn it into a model or statue.

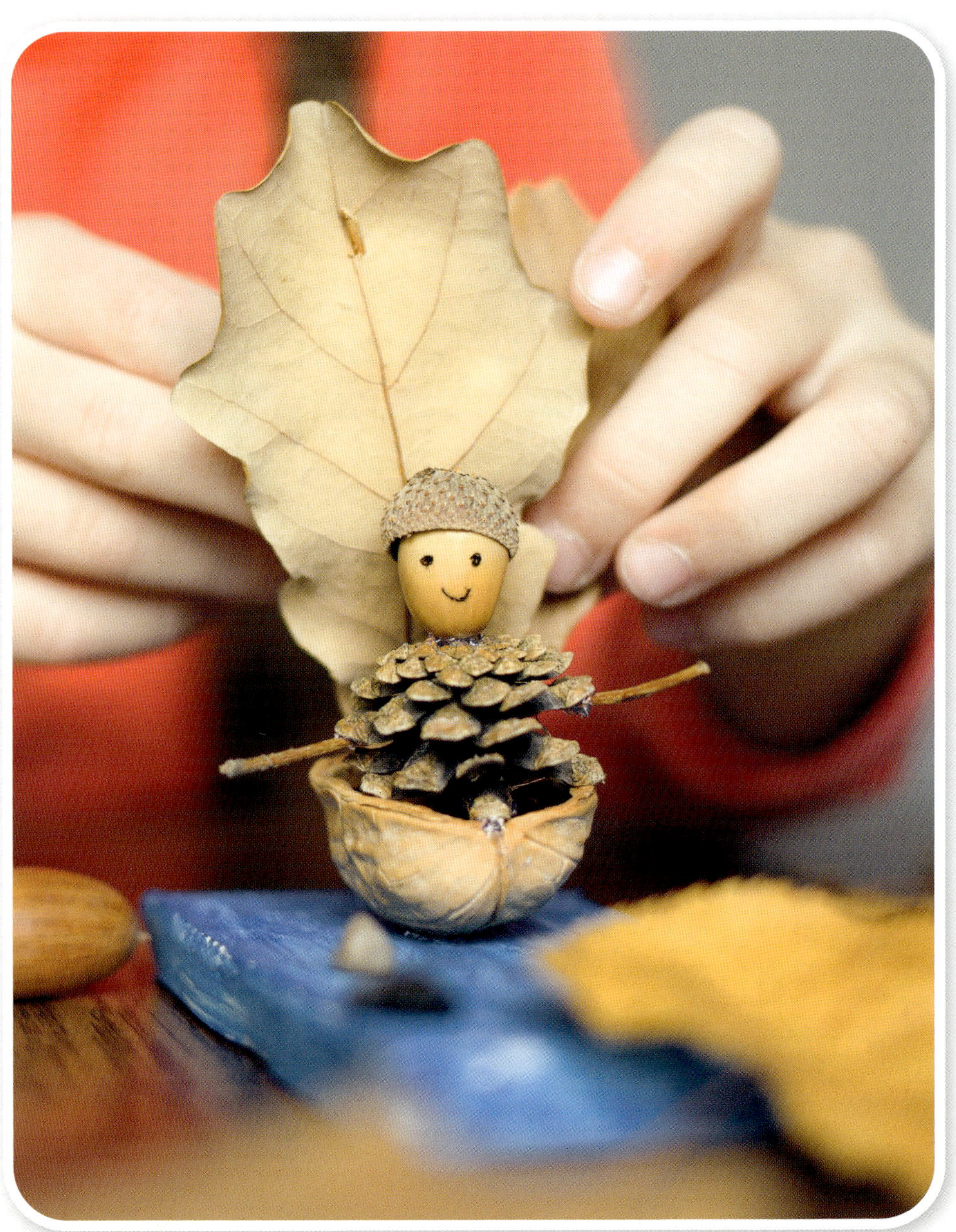

If you think art is fun, you could do it as a job when you are big!

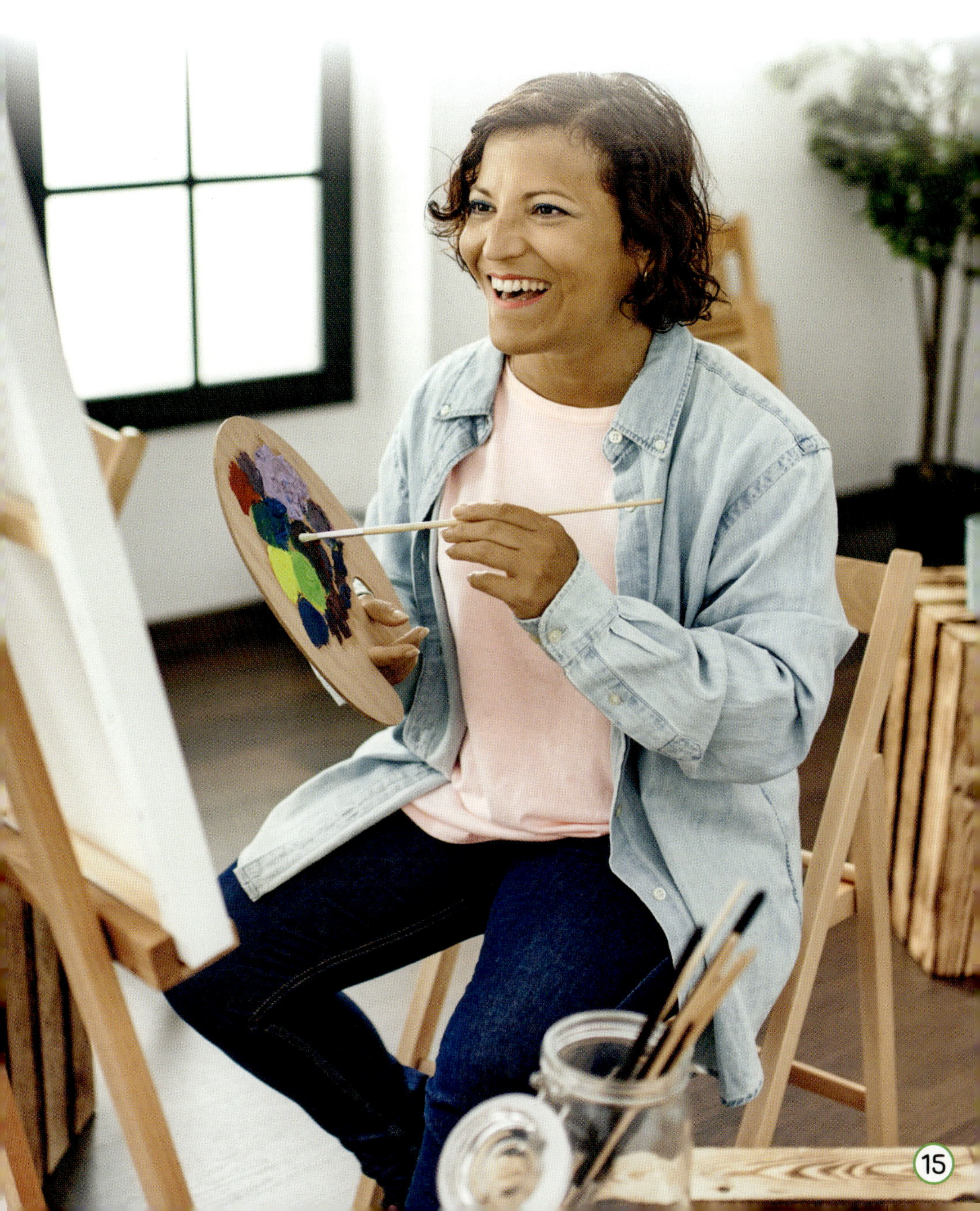

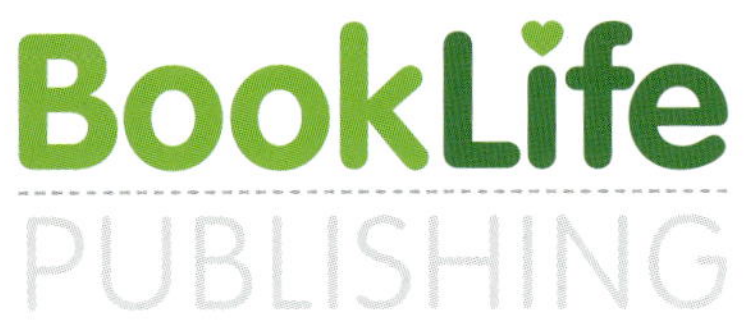

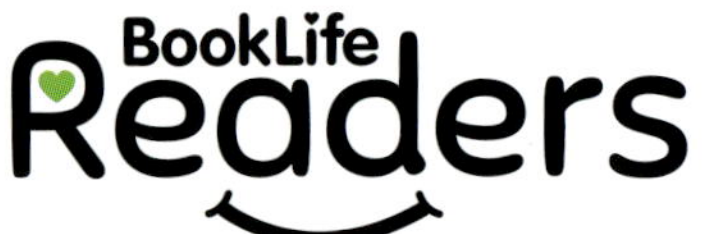

©2023 **BookLife Publishing Ltd.**
King's Lynn, Norfolk, PE30 4LS, UK.

ISBN 978-1-80505-065-0

All rights reserved. Printed in China.
A catalogue record for this book is
available from the British Library.

Art
Written by Charis Mather
Designed by Lucy Otter

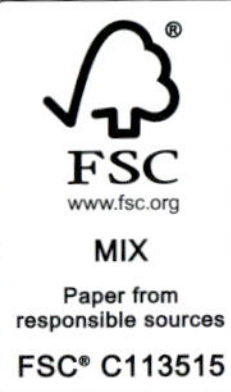

An Introduction to BookLife Readers...

Our Readers have been specifically created in line with the London Institute of Education's approach to book banding and are phonetically decodable and ordered to support each phase of the Letters and Sounds document.

Each book has been created to provide the best possible reading and learning experience. Our aim is to share our love of books with children, providing both emerging readers and prolific page-turners with beautiful books that are guaranteed to provoke interest and learning, regardless of ability.

BOOK BAND GRADED using the Institute of Education's approach to levelling.

PHONETICALLY DECODABLE supporting each phase of Letters and Sounds.

EXERCISES AND QUESTIONS to offer reinforcement and to ascertain comprehension.

CLEAR DESIGN to inspire and provoke engagement, providing the reader with clear visual representations of each non-fiction topic.

AUTHOR INSIGHT:
CHARIS MATHER

Charis Mather is a children's author at BookLife Publishing who has a love for reading and writing. Her studies in linguistics and experiences working with young readers have given her a knack for writing material that suits a range of ages and skill levels. Charis is passionate about producing books that emphasise the fun in reading and is convinced that no matter how much you already know, there is always something new to learn.

PHASE 5
/ue/aw/

This book focuses on /ue/ and /aw/ and is a Green level 5 book band.